Published by
Lion Publishing plc
Icknield Way, Tring, Herts, England
ISBN 0 7459 1002 5
Lion Publishing Corporation
10885 Textile Road, Belleville, Michigan 48111, USA
ISBN 0 7459 1002 5
Albatross Books Pty Ltd
PO Box 320, Sutherland, NSW 2232, Australia
ISBN 0 86760 648 7

First edition 1986

All the hymns and most of the extracts printed here
first appeared in the UK in *The Lion Book of Favourite Hymns*
and in the USA in *Stories of our Favorite Hymns*

Acknowledgments
Photographs by Sonia Halliday Photographs as follows:
F. H. C. Birch, 'A safe stronghold our God is still';
Sister Daniel, endpapers, 'All creatures of our God
and King', 'Holy, holy, holy', 'Let us, with a
gladsome mind', 'Joy to the World', 'Glory to thee,
my God, this night'; Sonia Halliday, 'O for a
thousand tongues to sing', 'The head that once
was crowned with thorns', 'Jesus lives!', 'Through all
the changing scenes of life', 'Who would true valour
see'; Laura Lushington, 'Lead us, heavenly
Father, lead us', 'What a Friend we have in Jesus',
'O come, O come, Emmanuel' and cover, 'Hark!
the herald angels sing'; Barrie Searle, 'Jesus loves me',
Else Trickett, 'All people that on earth do dwell',
'How sweet the name of Jesus sounds', 'And can it be',
'Take my life'

Printed and bound in Italy

SONGS OF FAITH

COMPILED BY CHRISTOPHER IDLE

A LION BOOK
Tring · Belleville · Sydney

ALL CREATURES
OF OUR GOD AND KING

Francis of Assisi was born into a wealthy
Italian family. His father, a cloth merchant, was furious when
Francis was converted to Jesus Christ and took seriously the
words in the Gospels about giving to the poor.

Turning his back on a life of luxury, Francis travelled
around the countryside with a few followers, preaching God's
love for every living creature. He loved God's world of nature
and saw all created things as objects of love which point to
their Creator. And in the growing cities, he preached the
gospel while living in utter poverty among ordinary people.

In the last year of his short life, ill, in pain and almost
blind, Francis wrote his *Canticle of the Sun*, beginning 'All
creatures of our God and King'. It was an early Italian version
of the church's *Benedicite* — 'O all ye works of the Lord, bless
ye the Lord'.

All creatures of our God and King,
Lift up your voice and with us sing
   Alleluia, Alleluia!
Thou burning sun with golden beam,
Thou silver moon with softer gleam:
O praise him, O praise him,
Alleluia, Alleluia, Alleluia!

Thou flowing water, pure and clear,
Make music for thy Lord to hear,
   Alleluia, Alleluia!
Thou fire so masterful and bright,
That givest man both warmth and
   light:

And all ye men of tender heart,
Forgiving others, take your part,
   O sing ye, Alleluia!
Ye who long pain and sorrow bear,
Praise God and on him cast your care;

Let all things their Creator bless,
And worship him in humbleness;
   O praise him, Alleluia!
Praise, praise the Father, praise the Son,
And praise the Spirit, Three in One;

FRANCIS OF ASSISI (1182–1226)
translated by WILLIAM DRAPER (1855–1933)

O FOR A THOUSAND TONGUES TO SING

Charles Wesley was never quite sure of his own birthday. It was, after all, just before Christmas; he was his mother's eighteenth child, born some weeks premature, so small and frail that he seemed more dead than alive. For two months he neither cried nor opened his eyes.

But he was quite sure of the date of what he called his 'second birth' — 21 May 1738. On that day he responded to the love and grace of God. He wrote this hymn a year later, 'For the anniversary day of one's conversion'.

O for a thousand tongues to sing
　My great Redeemer's praise,
The glories of my God and King,
　The triumphs of his grace!

Jesus! the name that charms our fears,
　That bids our sorrows cease;
'Tis music in the sinner's ears,
　'Tis life, and health, and peace.

He breaks the power of cancelled sin,
　He sets the prisoner free;
His blood can make the foulest clean,
　His blood availed for me.

He speaks, and, listening to his voice,
　New life the dead receive,
The mournful, broken hearts rejoice,
　The humble poor believe.

Hear him, ye deaf; his praise, ye dumb,
　Your loosened tongues employ;
Ye blind, behold your Saviour come,
　And leap, ye lame, for joy.

My gracious Master and my God,
　Assist me to proclaim,
To spread through all the earth abroad
　The honours of thy name.

CHARLES WESLEY (1707–88)

ALL PEOPLE
THAT ON EARTH DO DWELL

The Swiss city of Geneva conjures up different images for different people. Some may remember holidays among lake and mountain scenery; others think of the United Nations and international diplomacy. It has also come to stand for the religious tradition of the Puritans, and the historic 'Geneva Bible'.

Even in the sixteenth century, Geneva was a great 'united nations' — of refugees fleeing from religious persecution. Among them was Scotsman William Kethe, who shared in translating the Bible and wrote this enduring hymn, based on Psalm 100. Its famous tune, written by a Frenchman, is known as the 'Old Hundredth'.

All people that on earth do dwell,
Sing to the Lord with cheerful
voice;
Him serve with fear, his praise
forth tell,
Come ye before him, and rejoice.

The Lord, ye know, is God indeed,
Without our aid he did us make;
We are his folk, he doth us feed,
And for his sheep he doth us
take.

For why? the Lord our God is
good:
His mercy is for ever sure;
His truth at all times firmly stood,
And shall from age to age
endure.

O enter then his gates with praise,
Approach with joy his courts
unto;
Praise, laud, and bless his name
always,
For it is seemly so to do.

To Father, Son, and Holy Ghost,
The God whom heaven and
earth adore,
From men and from the angel-host
Be praise and glory evermore.

WILLIAM KETHE (d. 1594)

HOLY, HOLY, HOLY

'Dad, when was the first Trinity Sunday?'
Dad could not answer that perfectly serious and innocent question quite as easily as he could talk about the first Christmas or the first Easter.

Trinity Sunday is the one festival in the church's year marking not an event but a fact — the truth about the nature of God himself. And the words of 'Holy, holy, holy' stand almost alone among hymns; they simply attempt to describe, and worship, the three persons of the Godhead. Reginald Heber wrote them for one Trinity Sunday at his parish church in Shropshire.

When Heber was only forty, he became Bishop of Calcutta. But three years of travel and responsibility for the whole of India broke his health. Many of his stirring missionary hymns were published after his death.

Holy, Holy, Holy! Lord God
    Almighty!
  Early in the morning our song
    shall rise to thee;
Holy, Holy, Holy! Merciful and
    mighty!
  God in three Persons, blessed
    Trinity!

Holy, Holy, Holy! all the saints
    adore thee,
  Casting down their golden
    crowns around the glassy sea;
Cherubim and seraphim falling
    down before thee,
  Which wert, and art, and
    evermore shalt be.

Holy, Holy, Holy! though the
    darkness hide thee,
  Though the eye of sinful man
    thy glory may not see,
Only thou art holy, there is none
    beside thee
  Perfect in power, in love, and
    purity.

Holy, Holy, Holy! Lord God
    Almighty!
  All thy works shall praise thy
    name, in earth, and sky, and
    sea;
Holy, Holy, Holy! Merciful and
    mighty!
  God in three Persons, blessed
    Trinity!

REGINALD HEBER (1783–1826)

HOW SWEET
THE NAME OF JESUS SOUNDS

Neither John Newton's language nor his talent for verse had always been used for sacred purposes. In his early days on board ship, he taught the rest of the crew a song he had composed; what the lyrics said about the captain, his character, his family and his ship, was unprintable — like most of Newton's general conversation.

Another captain under whom he served was so appalled by Newton's constant blasphemy that when the weather turned stormy, he was convinced that he had a Jonah on board: Newton would have to go!

His conversion to Jesus Christ brought about startling changes for Newton, and this hymn is clear evidence that his mouth had had a spring-clean! He now used the name of Jesus in a new way, and his gift for choice words had been completely redirected.

How sweet the name of Jesus
    sounds
  In a believer's ear!
It soothes his sorrows, heals his
    wounds,
  And drives away his fear.

It makes the wounded spirit whole,
  And calms the troubled breast;
'Tis manna to the hungry soul,
  And to the weary rest.

Dear name! the rock on which I
    build,
  My shield and hiding-place,
My never-failing treasury filled
  With boundless stores of grace.

Jesus! my Shepherd, Husband,
    Friend,
  My Prophet, Priest, and King,
My Lord, my Life, my Way, my
    End,
  Accept the praise I bring.

Weak is the effort of my heart,
  And cold my warmest thought;
But when I see thee as thou art,
  I'll praise thee as I ought.

Till then I would thy love proclaim
  With every fleeting breath;
And may the music of thy name
  Refresh my soul in death.

JOHN NEWTON (1725–1807)

LET US,
WITH A GLADSOME MIND

'Either teach or learn, or leave': the motto, painted in Latin on the windows of St Paul's School in London, was hardly needed by John Milton, one of its brightest pupils.

He had 'a delicate, tuneable voice' and had inherited his father's love of music and books. He often sat up well after midnight to study Latin or Greek by candlelight. When he complained of headaches and tired eyes, no one recognized the warning signs; in his early forties he became totally blind.

Milton was fifteen, in his last year at St Paul's in 1623, when he wrote these lines. He put Psalm 136 into English verse, perhaps as a school exercise. This version makes him the youngest contributor to many hymn-books.

Let us, with a gladsome mind,
Praise the Lord, for he is kind:
For his mercies aye endure,
Ever faithful, ever sure.

Let us blaze his name abroad,
For of gods he is the God:

He with all-commanding might
Filled the new-made world with
   light:

Caused the golden-tressèd sun
All day long his course to run:

The hornèd moon to shine by night
'Mongst her spangled sisters bright:

He his chosen race did bless
In the wasteful wilderness:

He hath, with a piteous eye,
Looked upon our misery:

All things living he doth feed;
His full hand supplies their need:

Let us therefore warble forth
His great majesty and worth:

JOHN MILTON (1608–74)

A SAFE STRONGHOLD
OUR GOD IS STILL

Martin Luther was the leading figure of the Reformation of the church in Germany in the sixteenth century. As an obscure monk studying at a university, he rediscovered for himself that the only way to God was through faith in Jesus Christ.

It was a time when ordinary people were being promised a way out of hell if they would give money to rebuild St Peter's Church in Rome. Luther spoke out against such abuses. He was keen that people should read and understand the Bible for themselves, so he translated the New Testament from Greek into German. He introduced the German language into church services, which had previously been conducted in Latin. Luther also led the way in congregational hymn-singing, setting new words to the popular tunes of the day.

A safe stronghold our God is still,
  A trusty shield and weapon.
He'll help us clear from all the ill
  That hath us now o'ertaken.
    The ancient prince of hell
    Hath risen with purpose fell;
    Strong mail of craft and power
    He weareth in this hour;
On earth is not his fellow.

With force of arms we nothing can;
  Full soon were we down-ridden.
But for us fights the proper Man
  Whom God himself hath bidden.
    Ask ye, Who is this same?
    Christ Jesus is his name,
    The Lord Sabaoth's Son;
    He, and no other one,
Shall conquer in the battle.

And were this world all devils o'er,
  And watching to devour us.
We lay it not to heart so sore;
  Not they can overpower us.
    And let the prince of ill
    Look grim as e'er he will,
    He harms us not a whit;
    For why? his doom is writ —
A word shall quickly slay him.

God's word, for all their craft and
  force,
  One moment will not linger,
But, spite of hell, shall have its course;
  'Tis written by his finger.
    And though they take our life,
    Goods, honour, children, wife,
    Yet is their profit small;
    These things shall vanish all;
The City of God remaineth.

MARTIN LUTHER (1483–1546)
translated by THOMAS CARLYLE (1795–1881)

THE HEAD THAT ONCE
WAS CROWNED WITH THORNS

Thomas Kelly was the son of an Irish judge. He was ordained but fell foul of his bishop and founded his own sect, which nearly died with him. But this hymn has stood the test of time.

Kelly's practical faith was put to the test during a year of severe famine. He was loved by the poorest of the people for his kindness. One man cheered up his anxious wife by saying, 'Hold up, Bridget — there's always Mister Kelly to pull us out of the mire after we've sunk for the last time!'

The head that once was crowned
    with thorns
  Is crowned with glory now:
A royal diadem adorns
  The mighty Victor's brow.

The highest place that heaven
    affords
  Is his, is his by right,
The King of kings and Lord of
    lords,
  And heaven's eternal Light;

The joy of all who dwell above,
  The joy of all below,
To whom he manifests his love,
  And grants his name to know.

To them the cross, with all its
    shame,
  With all its grace is given:
Their name an everlasting name,
  Their joy the joy of heaven.

They suffer with their Lord below,
  They reign with him above,
Their profit and their joy to know
  The mystery of his love.

The cross he bore is life and health,
  Though shame and death to
    him;
His people's hope, his people's
    wealth,
  Their everlasting theme.

THOMAS KELLY (1769–1855)

JESUS LIVES!

The German Lutheran who wrote this hymn was known for his bad memory — and his generous spirit.

As assistant pastor to his father, he could not remember his own sermons well enough to preach without notes — and reading the sermon was frowned on. So he became a lecturer instead, and as Professor of Philosophy he filled his lecture-room to overflowing.

His kindness overflowed too. He gave away so much that when Prince Henry of Prussia visited him, he found him living in one empty room without food or fire. But, if only with this one Easter hymn, he has made many others rich.

Jesus lives! thy terrors now
Can, O death, no more appal us;
Jesus lives! by this we know
Thou, O grave, canst not
enthral us. Alleluia!

Jesus lives! henceforth is death
But the gate of life immortal;
This shall calm our trembling
breath,
When we pass its gloomy
portal. Alleluia!

Jesus lives! for us he died;
Then, alone, to Jesus living,
Pure in heart may we abide,
Glory to our Saviour giving.
Alleluia!

Jesus lives! our hearts know well
Nought from us his love shall
sever;
Life, nor death, nor powers of hell
Tear us from his keeping ever.
Alleluia!

Jesus lives! to him the throne
Over all the world is given;
May we go where he is gone,
Rest and reign with him in
heaven. Alleluia!

CHRISTIAN GELLERT (1715–69)
translated by FRANCES COX (1812–97)

AND CAN IT BE

In spite of their differing temperaments, brothers John and Charles Wesley did many things together. At Oxford they formed the 'Holy Club' and earned the name of 'Methodist'; in Georgia they were none-too-successful missionaries; in London in 1738 they each found the experience that brought them peace with God. They also published hymn-books together. Although no one is quite sure which of the brothers wrote this hymn, Charles usually gets the credit.

He was converted to a living, personal faith while staying with a brazier called John Bray, who lived almost under the shadow of St Paul's Cathedral. On the Sunday when his 'chains fell off', Charles read in his *Book of Common Prayer* from Psalm 40: 'He hath put a new song in my mouth: even a thanksgiving unto our God.'

For the man who wrote nearly 7,000 new songs of praise to God, those were prophetic words.

And can it be that I should gain
  An interest in the Saviour's
    blood?
Died he for me, who caused his
    pain?
  For me, who him to death
    pursued?
Amazing love! how can it be
That thou, my God, shouldst die
    for me!

He left his Father's throne above,
  So free, so infinite his grace,
Emptied himself of all but love,
  And bled for Adam's helpless
    race.
'Tis mercy all, immense and free;
For, O my God, it found out me!

Long my imprisoned spirit lay
  Fast bound in sin and nature's
    night;
Thine eye diffused a quickening ray —
  I woke, the dungeon flamed
    with light;
My chains fell off, my heart was free,
I rose, went forth, and followed
    thee.

No condemnation now I dread;
  Jesus, and all in him, is mine!
Alive in him, my living head,
  And clothed in righteousness
    divine,
Bold I approach the eternal throne,
And claim the crown, through
    Christ, my own.

CHARLES WESLEY (1707–88)

JESUS LOVES ME

In October 1949 Chairman Mao Tse Tung declared the establishment of the People's Republic of China. It quickly became apparent that all western Christians would have to leave the country. Soon mainland China was closed to Christians outside.

The church in China went through a very hard time. The little news that did leak out had to be discreet. And in one message received in 1972, there was a sentence which read, 'The *this I know* people are well.'

To the authorities the words did not make sense. But such is the international language of Christian songs that friends outside the bamboo curtain knew immediately that their fellow-believers were in good heart.

Jesus loves me, this I know,
For the Bible tells me so;
Little ones to him belong,
They are weak, but he is strong.

Jesus loves me! He who died
Heaven's gate to open wide;
He will wash away my sin,
Let his little child come in.

Yes, Jesus loves me;
    yes, Jesus loves me;
Yes, Jesus loves me,
    the Bible tells me so.

ANNA WARNER (1820–1915)

TAKE MY LIFE

Frances Ridley Havergal was a natural musician and could have been a professional singer. She was not strong physically — she 'hoped the angels would have orders to let her alone a bit when she first got to heaven' — but she worked hard and used her musical and linguistic gifts to the full. This hymn was written on the last night of a five-day visit to a friend's home, where she wanted everyone to commit themselves wholeheartedly to God and experience his blessings.

She lived out the words in her hymns, too. She once wrote to another friend: ' "Take my silver and my gold" now means shipping off all my ornaments — including a jewel cabinet which is really fit for a countess — to the Church Missionary Society . . . I retain only a brooch for daily wear, which is a memorial of my dear parents; also a locket . . . I had no idea I had such a jeweller's shop . . . I don't think I need tell you I never packed a box with such pleasure.'

Take my life, and let it be
Consecrated, Lord, to thee;
Take my moments and my days,
Let them flow in ceaseless praise.

Take my hands, and let them move
At the impulse of thy love.
Take my feet, and let them be
Swift and beautiful for thee.

Take my voice, and let me sing
Always, only, for my King;
Take my lips, and let them be
Filled with messages from thee.

Take my silver and my gold;
Not a mite would I withhold;
Take my intellect, and use
Every power as thou shalt choose.

Take my will, and make it thine:
It shall be no longer mine.
Take my heart; it is thine own:
It shall be thy royal throne.

Take my love; my Lord, I pour
At thy feet its treasure-store.
Take myself, and I will be
Ever, only, all, for thee.

FRANCES RIDLEY HAVERGAL (1836–79)

LEAD US,
HEAVENLY FATHER, LEAD US

If James Edmeston were to return to his native east London today — he was born at Wapping and died at Hackney — he would not easily recognize his surroundings. New housing estates and tower blocks have taken over where bombs fell or old buildings crumbled. It is even less likely that he would see many of the buildings which he, as an architect and surveyor, designed. However, the parish church of St Barnabas still stands in Homerton High Street. Edmeston was churchwarden there for many years.

This hymn, among 2,000 others he wrote, has outlived any of his environmental achievements and is now firmly established as a favourite choice at wedding services.

Lead us, heavenly Father, lead us
    O'er the world's tempestuous
    sea;
Guard us, guide us, keep us, feed
    us,
    For we have no help but thee;
Yet possessing every blessing
    If our God our Father be.

Saviour, breathe forgiveness o'er us,
    All our weakness thou dost
    know,
Thou didst tread this earth before us,
    Thou didst feel its keenest woe;
Son of Mary, lone and weary,
    Victor through this world
    didst go.

Spirit of our God, descending,
    Fill our hearts with heavenly joy,
Love with every passion blending,
    Pleasure that can never cloy:
Thus provided, pardoned, guided,
    Nothing can our peace destroy.

JAMES EDMESTON (1791–1867)

THROUGH ALL
THE CHANGING SCENES OF LIFE

'Tate and Brady' were once as familiar and inseparable a pair of names as Laurel and Hardy or Rodgers and Hammerstein.

They were Irish Protestants whose *New Version* of metrical psalms, published in 1696, replaced the so-called *Old Version* of the previous generation. This version of part of Psalm 34 is the one survivor that has stayed the course for nearly three centuries.

But new versions always have their critics. Brady's own church would have none of it; to them it was 'an innovation not to be endured'. And Tate's brother had a maid who refused to come to family prayers because of it. 'As long as you sang Jesus Christ's psalms, I sung along with ye,' she said. 'But now that you sing psalms of your own invention, ye may sing by yourselves!'

Through all the changing scenes of life,
In trouble and in joy,
The praises of my God shall still
My heart and tongue employ.

O magnify the Lord with me,
With me exalt his name;
When in distress to him I called,
He to my rescue came.

The hosts of God encamp around
The dwellings of the just;
Deliverance he affords to all
Who on his succour trust.

O make but trial of his love,
Experience will decide
How blest they are, and only they,
Who in his truth confide.

Fear him, ye saints, and you will then
Have nothing else to fear;
Make you his service your delight,
Your wants shall be his care.

NAHUM TATE (1652–1715)
NICHOLAS BRADY (1659–1726)

WHAT A FRIEND
WE HAVE IN JESUS

On the eve of Joseph Scriven's intended wedding-day, his bride-to-be was tragically drowned. Later he emigrated from Ireland to Canada. Once again he became engaged to be married, only to lose his second fiancée after a brief but fatal illness.

In spite of loneliness, poverty and his own precarious health, he spent the rest of his life helping the physically handicapped, as well as teaching and ministering among his fellow Christian Brethren in Ontario.

But it was not his own troubles that led him to write this hymn. He sent the words to his mother when she was going through a very distressing time. So, as with many other hymns, a private message has become a source of comfort to people across the world.

What a Friend we have in Jesus
 All our sins and griefs to bear;
What a privilege to carry
 Everything to God in prayer.
O what peace we often forfeit,
 O what needless pain we bear;
All because we do not carry
 Everything to God in prayer.

Have we trials and temptations?
 Is there trouble anywhere?
We should never be discouraged;
 Take it to the Lord in prayer.
Can we find a friend so faithful
 Who will all our sorrows share?
Jesus knows our every weakness;
 Take it to the Lord in prayer.

Are we weak and heavy-laden,
 Cumbered with a load of care?
Precious Saviour, still our refuge —
 Take it to the Lord in prayer.
Do thy friends despise, forsake thee?
 Take it to the Lord in prayer;
In his arms he'll take and shield thee,
 Thou wilt find a solace there.

JOSEPH MEDLICOTT SCRIVEN (1819–86)

WHO WOULD
TRUE VALOUR SEE

Christiana and her four sons are nearing the goal of the pilgrimage when they meet a wounded man on the road. His name is Mr Valiant-for-Truth. They wash his wounds, give him food and drink, and learn his story as they travel on together.

Spurred on by the example of Christian himself, Mr Valiant-for-Truth had set out on the journey from the City of Destruction to the Celestial City. He relates the obstacles and battles along the way and, since pilgrims love to sing, launches into 'Who would true valour see . . .'

This is just a part of John Bunyan's masterpiece, *The Pilgrim's Progress*, an allegory of a Christian's spiritual pilgrimage. Now a classic of English literature, it was written while Bunyan was imprisoned in Bedford jail. He was persecuted for his faith and his preaching — but though his voice was silenced for a while, his pen was not.

> Who would true valour see,
>   Let him come hither;
> One here will constant be,
>   Come wind, come weather.
> There's no discouragement
> Shall make him once relent
> His first avowed intent
>   To be a pilgrim.

> Who so beset him round
>   With dismal stories,
> Do but themselves confound;
>   His strength the more is.
> No lion can him fright,
> He'll with a giant fight,
> But he will have a right
>   To be a pilgrim.

> Hobgoblin nor foul fiend
>   Can daunt his spirit;
> He knows he at the end
>   Shall life inherit.
> Then fancies fly away;
> He'll fear not what men say;
> He'll labour night and day
>   To be a pilgrim.

JOHN BUNYAN (1628–88)

O COME,
O COME, EMMANUEL

John Mason Neale was a born scholar. Before he was ten, he edited his own handwritten family magazine. As a shy but strong-minded young man, he could often be seen making a brass-rubbing or collecting architectural details in country churches he visited on his walking-tours.

He grew up to love the Middle Ages and the medieval church, the early church fathers and the lives of the saints. One small girl at his orphanage said that Mr Neale (then in his forties) 'must be very old, to have talked to so many saints and martyrs'.

This Advent hymn is from a Latin original of doubtful date. As the greatest of all translators of hymns, Neale helped to disprove his friend Benjamin Webb's words: 'I am more and more convinced that the age of hymns has passed'!

O come, O come, Emmanuel,
And ransom captive Israel.
That mourns in lonely exile here,
Until the Son of God appear.
Rejoice! Rejoice! Emmanuel
Shall come to thee, O Israel.

O come, thou Rod of Jesse, free
Thine own from Satan's tyranny;
From depths of hell thy people save,
And give them victory o'er the grave.

O come, thou Dayspring, come
   and cheer
Our spirits by thine advent here;
Disperse the gloomy clouds of night,
And death's dark shadows put to
   flight.

O come, thou Key of David, come,
And open wide our heavenly home;
Make safe the way that leads on
   high,
And close the path to misery.

O come, O come, thou Lord of
   Might,
Who to thy tribes, on Sinai's height,
In ancient times didst give the law
In cloud and majesty and awe.

From the Latin; translated by JOHN MASON NEALE (1818–66)

JOY TO THE WORLD!
THE LORD IS COME!

As the world's leading gospel singer prior to her death in 1972, Mahalia Jackson mixed with princesses and presidents, film-stars and top entertainers. But she turned down countless lucrative offers from bars, night-clubs and theatres — anywhere that liquor was sold. And she never sang the blues, considering it 'Devil's music'.

As a child in the poverty of New Orleans, Mahalia started singing. 'Hand me down my silver trumpet, Gabriel' was a life-long favourite, but so were the 'old Dr Watts' hymns of her Baptist church.

One Christmas, a blizzard stopped her going from Chicago to Memphis, where she was due to sing for civil rights workers in the negro college. So she called the telephone company, and from 8358 Indiana she held the 'phone for half an hour, and sang: 'Born in Bethlehem', 'Silent Night' and the 'old Dr Watts' — 'Joy to the World!'

Joy to the world! the Lord is come!
  Let earth receive her King!
Let every heart prepare him room,
  And heaven and nature sing.

Joy to the earth! the Saviour reigns!
  Let men their songs employ!
While fields and floods, rocks,
    hills, and plains
  Repeat the sounding joy.

No more let sins and sorrows grow,
  Nor thorns infest the ground;
He comes to make his blessings flow
  Far as the curse is found.

He rules the world with truth and
    grace,
  And makes the nations prove
The glories of his righteousness,
  And wonders of his love.

ISAAC WATTS (1674–1748)

HARK!
THE HERALD-ANGELS SING

On Christmas Day 1738, Charles Wesley
preached at St Mary's Church in Islington, and gave the wine
at Holy Communion. Next day it was George Whitefield's
turn. 'We had the sacrament this and the four following days
— the whole week was a festival indeed; a joyful season, holy
unto the Lord.'

Was that the first Christmas ever to be enriched by this
hymn? In its original version, it was published a few months
later; Whitefield was one of those who afterwards shaped it to
its present form.

So whenever we sing these words today, we are heirs to the
work of England's finest hymn-writer and her greatest
preacher.

The composer Mendelssohn belongs to the next century,
but he did not live long enough to hear his famous music
matched with this magnificent hymn.

Hark! the herald-angels sing
Glory to the new-born King,
Peace on earth, and mercy mild,
God and sinners reconciled.
Joyful, all ye nations, rise,
Join the triumph of the skies;
With the angelic host proclaim
'Christ is born in Bethlehem.'
Hark! the herald-angels sing
Glory to the new-born King.

Christ, by highest heaven adored,
Christ, the everlasting Lord,
Late in time behold him come,
Offspring of a virgin's womb.
Veiled in flesh the Godhead see!
Hail, the incarnate Deity!
Pleased as Man with man to dwell,
Jesus, our Emmanuel.

Hail, the heaven-born Prince of Peace!
Hail, the Sun of Righteousness!
Light and life to all he brings,
Risen with healing in his wings.
Mild he lays his glory by,
Born that man no more may die,
Born to raise the sons of earth,
Born to give them second birth.

CHARLES WESLEY (1707–88) and others

GLORY TO THEE,
MY GOD, THIS NIGHT

Thomas Ken wrote these words for the boys of Winchester College. A pastor at heart, he disliked controversy. But he felt he had to cross swords with three successive kings of England on matters of principle.

While at Winchester, he refused to put his house at the disposal of Nell Gwyn, mistress of Charles II, during a royal visit. But Charles bore no malice; when the bishopric of Bath and Wells fell vacant, he said, 'Where is the little fellow who refused poor Nelly a lodging? Give it to him!'

Ken remained a loyal bishop under James II; but he resisted the monarch's increasingly illegal measures, to the point of being imprisoned in the Tower of London. And when William and Mary came to the throne, he would not take the Oath of Allegiance. Because he considered that his oath to the exiled James still held good, he was deprived of his position in the church and in public life.

Glory to thee, my God, this night
For all the blessings of the light;
Keep me, O keep me, King of kings,
Under thy own almighty wings.

Forgive me, Lord, for thy dear Son,
The ill that I this day have done,
That with the world, myself, and thee,
I, e'er I sleep, at peace may be.

Teach me to live, that I may dread
The grave as little as my bed;
Teach me to die, that so I may
Triumphing rise at the last day.

O may my soul on thee repose,
And with sweet sleep mine eyelids close —
Sleep that may me more vigorous make
To serve my God when I awake.

When in the night I sleepless lie,
My soul with heavenly thoughts supply;
Let no ill dreams disturb my rest,
No powers of darkness me molest.

Praise God from whom all blessings flow,
Praise him, all creatures here below;
Praise him above, ye heavenly host,
Praise Father, Son, and Holy Ghost.

THOMAS KEN (1637–1711)